Brewster: The Way We Were

by George H. Boyd III

A Pictorial History of Brewster, Massachusetts
from old postcards contained in the collection of The Brewster Store

Knowles' Store, Brewster, Mass.

The author wishes to thank Joe Hughes for sharing his collection of old post-cards. Several pictures from cards in his collection are included in this book. Ellen St. Sure, the Archivist of the Town of Brewster, provided considerable assistance on historical facts about Brewster as well as the editing of the text, for which I am most grateful. Various other people, too numerous to mention here, contributed their insights for which I am extremely thankful.

This book is dedicated to my wife Missy who provided both encouragement and editing – and who lured me to Brewster over forty years ago.

Published by George H. Boyd III

Copyright 2016 by George H. Boyd III

All rights reserved.
Published 2016.

ISBN 978-0-9978182-0-8

George H. Boyd III
1935 Main Street, Brewster, MA 02632
email: gboyd@nyc.rr.com
www.brewsterstore.com

This book was designed and typeset by Nancy Viall Shoemaker of West Barnstable Press, West Barnstable, Massachusetts.

The fonts used were Classical Garamond for the text and Goudy in the chapter heads. The postmark notations were set in Optima, while the photo credits are in Frutiger.

Brewster: The Way We Were was printed on 100 lb. white matte coated.

TABLE OF CONTENTS

The Brewster Store Postcard Collection

Today the Town of Brewster contains almost 300 homes and buildings which were initially constructed prior to 1925 – several before 1700. The Brewster Store has a large collection of postcards and photos that document Brewster through images starting shortly after the turn of the 20th Century. Many of the earliest ones were actually published by W. W. Knowles & Son, the second name of the Brewster Store, titled after its owners. We have decided to publish a selection of the Store's postcards to provide a visual record of Brewster's past – its homes, businesses and churches – as well as to provide a view of its beaches and countryside, the latter denuded of its trees for farm land and for heating the homes of earlier citizens. The largest number of postcards of individual buildings were of the old mill, the beaches, the Sea Pines School for Girls and the Nickerson Estate. We continue to welcome contributions to our collection of old photographs or postcards of Brewster to add to this documentation of Brewster's past. Unless otherwise noted on the picture, the postcards and photographs in this book were originally published by W. W. Knowles and Son or there was no attribution to a publisher. Below are two old postcard images of Main Street when it was a dirt road, to the east and west of The Brewster Store.

Brief History of Postcards

Until the middle of the 19th century, people mailed messages to each other via the privacy of sealed letters. The idea for the postal card originated in Germany in 1865. It was the Austrian government, however, that on October 1, 1869, issued the first postal card. The early postal cards had their critics. Many people thought it was improper to mail messages on cards that anyone, especially the servants, could read. Because postal cards could be mailed for much less postage than the normal letter rate, however, they soon became a hit with the general public.

The U. S. Post Office was the only establishment allowed to print postcards in The United States; the Post Office Department issued America's first postal card on May 13, 1873. It held its monopoly until May 19, 1898, when Congress passed the Private Mailing Card Act. This allowed private publishers and printers to produce postcards. Initially, the United States government prohibited private companies from calling their cards "postcards", so they were known as "souvenir cards." These cards had to be labeled "Private Mailing Cards." This prohibition was rescinded on December 24, 1901, when private companies could use the word "postcard."

Postcards were not allowed to have a divided back and correspondents could only write on the front of the postcard. This was known as the "undivided back" era of postcards. Several postcards in the collection of the Brewster Store are from this era.

On March 1, 1907 the Post Office allowed private citizens to write on the address side of a postcard and allowed to have a "divided back." On these cards the back is divided into two sections, the left section for the message and the right for the address. Thus began the Golden Age of American postcards, which peaked in 1910 with the introduction of tariffs on German-printed postcards and ended by 1915 when World War I ultimately disrupted the printing and import of the fine-printed cards. Many postcards of Brewster were produced in Germany, including the one below.

Street Scene,
East Brewster, Mass.

E.F. Hamblin

Between 1907 and 1910 postcards were particularly popular among rural and small-town women in the northern United States. In 1908, more than 677 million postcards were mailed. The "white border" era in postcards named for the obvious reason, lasted from about 1916 to the 1930's.

The last and current postcard era "chrome" began about 1939, although these cards did not begin to dominate until about 1950. The images or chrome cards are generally based on colored photographs and are readily identified by the glossy appearance of the paper's coating. There are only a few of these "chrome" cards in this book and only where the subject did not exist until after World War II. The Brewster Store postcard collection has many black and white cards from the 1940's.

The Brewster Store was originally built as the second Unitarian Church in 1852 on a knoll overlooking Carlton E. Sears Square at the intersection of the Old King's Highway and the Old Harwich Road (pictured at right). The building served on and off as a church until 1865 when W. W. Knowles purchased it and changed it into a general store. The steeple was removed and sold, the ceiling of the first floor was raised; large windows and a porch were added to the front of the building. In the Spring of 1866 Knowles moved his goods from his first general store to the east on Main Street into this larger structure. He opened his new store in the summer of 1866. Upstairs was the "Hall" which served for many years as a venue for Brewster School graduations, dances and parties.

The Postcard Tour of Brewster

This picture book starts the tour of Brewster Village at the center of the town–the area around The Brewster Store, then moves west to Tubman Road along Main Street. It then reverses, proceeding east down the Old King's Highway which today is known as Route 6A, diverting south down Underpass Road to the Old Chatham Road (Route 137) and the surrounding area. The next segment–East Brewster–stretches from Underpass Road along Route 6A to Nickerson State Park. This is followed by a tour west along the beaches bordering Cape Cod Bay. Following the beaches it circles back to west of The Brewster Store down Route 6A and up Stony Brook Road and West Brewster returning to Route 6A and heading back east toward the center of town along Lower Road to Brewster Park.

Walker Barnstable County Atlas

The next two pages contain portions of the Atlas of Barnstable Count published in 1880 by George W. Walker & Co. It is replete with maps of each of the sixteen towns of Cape Cod with the locations and names of the owners of most of the homes and businesses. The map of Brewster was divided into three sections–the Village of Brewster, East Brewster and West Brewster. The village of Brewster extended along the Old King's Highway (now alternatively known as Main Street or Route 6A) from about Tubman Road on the west to Underpass Road to the east. The villages of East and West Brewster extended out from the center of town in their respective compass directions along Main Street. From a postal perspective, until 1928 the town was divided into five separate areas, each served by its own post office. One each for the above three portions of the town plus South Brewster, along the Old Chatham Road (now Route 137) that centered on the main Brewster train depot. The fifth was the North Brewster Post Office, covering the area from the intersection of Stony Brook Road and Route 6A, west to the Brewster town line.

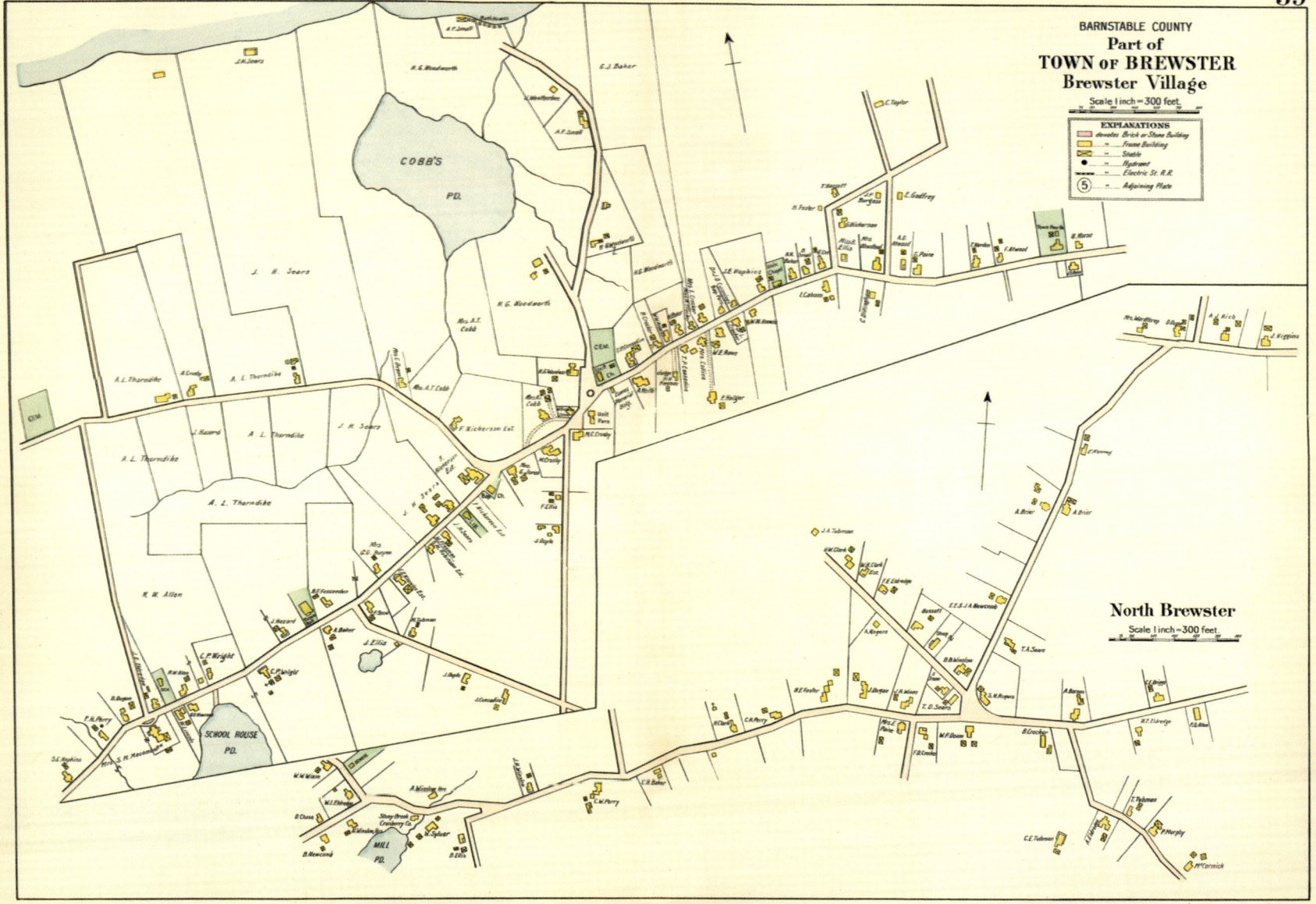

39

BARNSTABLE COUNTY
Part of
TOWN OF BREWSTER
Brewster Village
Scale 1 inch = 300 feet.

EXPLANATIONS
□ denotes Brick or Stone Building
□ " " Frame Building
□ " " Stable
● " " Hydrant
" " Electric St. R.R.
(5) " " Adjoining Plate

COBB'S PD.

North Brewster
Scale 1 inch = 300 feet.

SCHOOL HOUSE PD.

MILL PD.

BREWSTER: *The Way We Were*

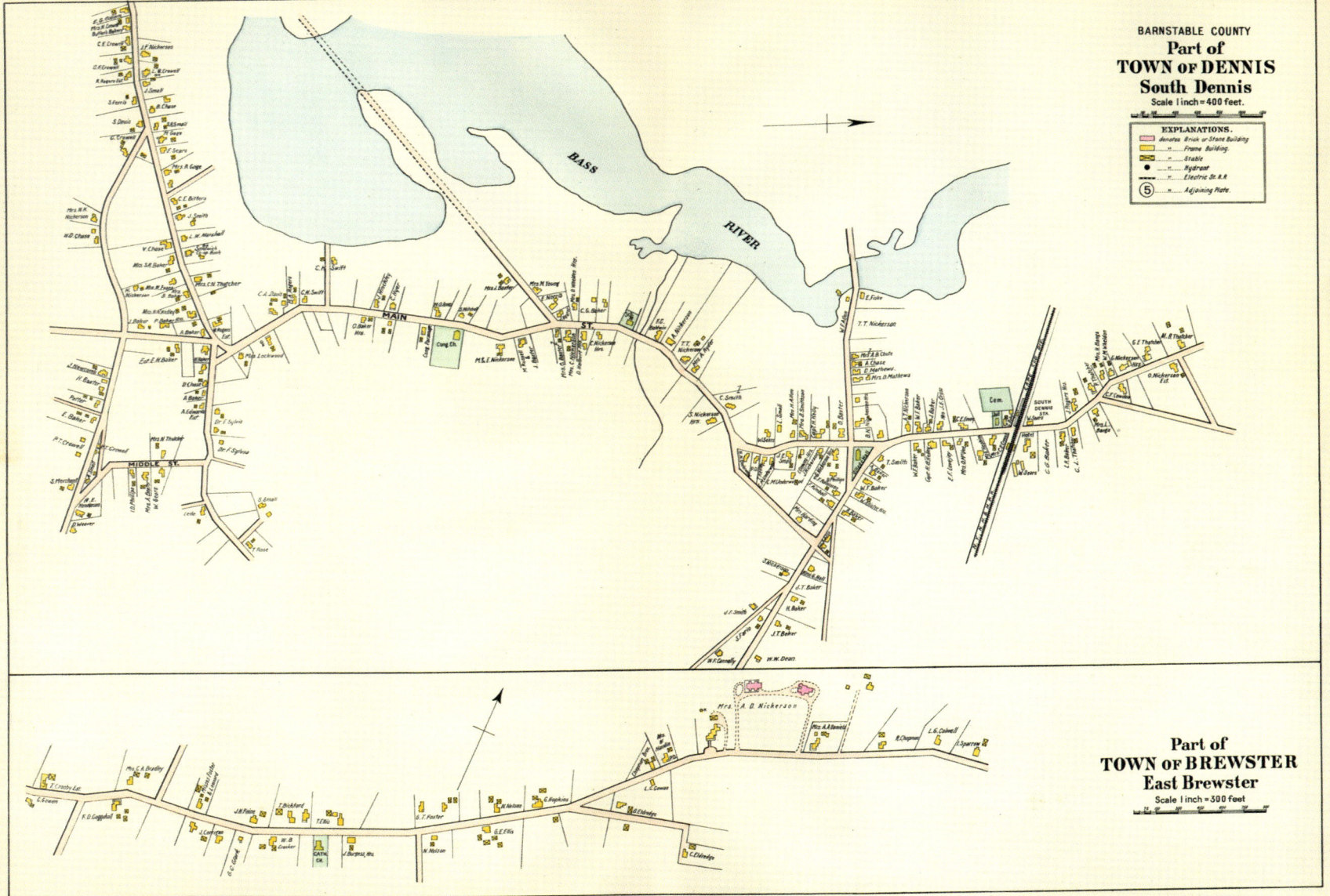

BARNSTABLE COUNTY
Part of
TOWN of DENNIS
South Dennis
Scale 1 inch = 400 feet.

EXPLANATIONS.

BASS

RIVER

MAIN

ST.

MIDDLE ST.

Cem.

SOUTH DENNIS STA.

Part of
TOWN of BREWSTER
East Brewster
Scale 1 inch = 300 feet

Brewster Village

This is a view of the W. W. Knowles and Son store with W. W. standing in front with the oil lamp, which dates the photograph sometime between 1884 and 1904 when William passed away. The lamp and post in front of the Brewster Store were initially installed by Knowles in November, 1884, following his appointment as postmaster in 1883. This improvement to the town was acknowledged in an article in the November 11, 1884 *Barnstable Patriot*.

"It is pleasant to welcome the improvements made by the promptings of Public Spirit. Our enterprising citizen, W. W. Knowles, has furnished two street lamps to make more attractive our thoroughfares; one of them makes brilliant the square (Carlton E. Square) in front of the store and the other stands before his dwelling (now the Bramble Inn) to cheer the traveller's way. A few more such are still needed; and the benevolent are invited to improve the hint. Does not the apostle advise that 'we provoke one another to good works.'"

signed T.D.

The Knowles Store, built as a church in 1852, was located on an intersection that was known early on as the Carlton E. Sears Square. This was the view from the Store's front porch out over Main Street and the

Old Harwich Road. Behind the automobiles is the home built by Captain Judah P. Baker. By 1880 the home was owned by Tully Crosby Jr. Still standing today, the house was built sometime around 1850.

West of the Knowles Store stood the home of Freeman Cobb pictured to the left, courtesy of the late Mr. Henry Allen. The house was built in 1859, with the wealth Cobb had accumulated in Australia providing supplies to the gold fields.

The house was dismantled in 1950 and replaced in 1951 by the family home which still stands on the same footprint. The original carriage barn still remains; it was converted into a summer cottage in 1922.

Just to the west of the Cobb estate is the intersection of the Old Kings Highway and Lower Road. In the background can be seen the former residence of Captain Winslow L. Knowles who purchased it in 1845. It was sold to Frederick Nickerson after Knowles' death in 1873. The house was apparently built prior to 1789. More recently the home has been converted into an inn and is now called the Old Manse Inn.

Main St. Brewster Mass. "The Corner"

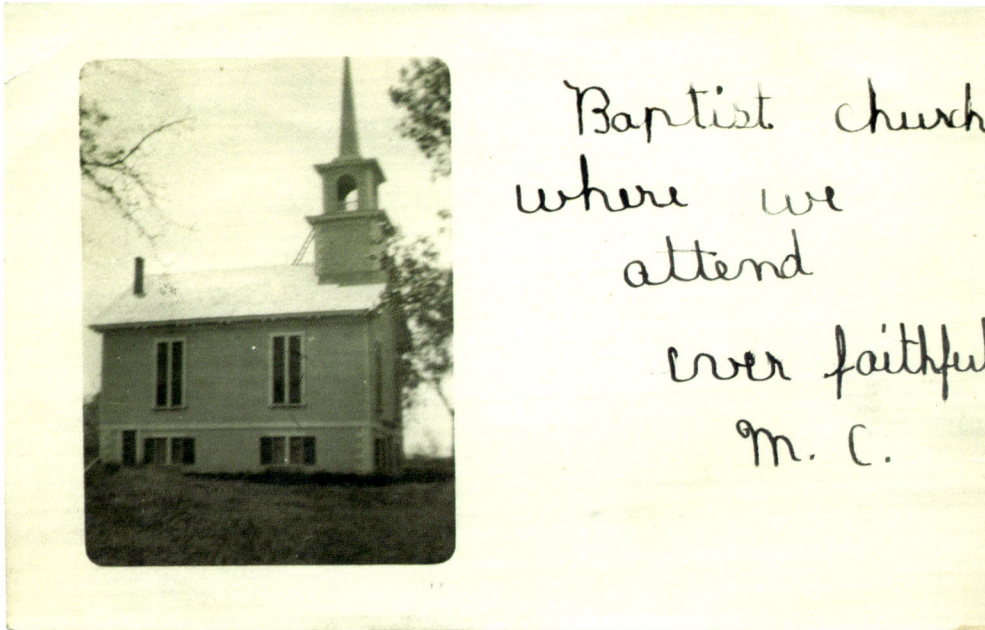

Baptist church where we attend ever faithful M. C.

Across the street from the Winslow Knowles home is the Brewster Baptist Church organized in 1824 and pictured here in a 1905 postcard. The first meeting house was built in 1828 near the one pictured, which was erected in 1860. Its tall tapered steeple was damaged by a fire in 1881 and replaced with the shorter one pictured. In 1912 a third squat steeple tower was installed. The church replaced it in 2015 with one thought to be similar to the original.

Ladies Library
Brewster Mass.

Just west of the Baptist Church is the Brewster Ladies Library, founded in 1852 by a dozen local ladies each contributing two books and one dollar. With gifts from many townspeople, the library opened on January 29, 1853. In 1864 Captain Tully Crosby and Dr. S. H. Gould gave the land; Joseph Nickerson donated $1,000. This building opened in January 24, 1868. The above picture from a postcard mailed in 1909 included an addition built in 1877. Since then the building has been dramatically enlarged, the latest addition built in 1997.

To the right is an early postcard picture of the birthplace of Joseph C. Lincoln (1870-1944), famed Cape Cod author, just a few steps west of the Brewster Ladies Library. He lived here until 1883. His father was a Cape Cod sea captain who died when Joseph was ten months old. The home was previously owned by his mother's family, the Crosbys, and built prior to 1850 with a shoemaker's shop next door. Ancestors on both sides of the family settled on Cape Cod in the mid 17th century. Joseph Lincoln's many stories, primarily built around Cape Cod surroundings, were printed in books and *The Saturday Evening Post*.

BIRTHPLACE OF JOSEPH C. LINCOLN (WRITER OF CAPE COD STORIES), BREWSTER, CAPE COD, MASS.

BREWSTER GARAGE, BREWSTER, MASS.

The Brewster garage building is still located on the corner of Main Street and the Old Chatham Road (now Rt. 137). It was built sometime after 1910 to accommodate the growing onslaught of the automobile. "If you stopped for gas at the Brewster Garage, you would be met by Agathe Gervais, who would emerge from the gray shingled building carrying a wooden step-stool. Miss Gervais, a petite woman who ran the garage into her eighties, needed the stool to reach the windshield, which she carefully cleaned. When she wasn't changing oil in grimy engines, Miss Gervais was a concert pianist. She was also a champion talker. Sometimes a customer would attempt to break away by starting the car, but Agathe would walk along with the moving vehicle if she hadn't finished her tale yet." This quote is from a forthcoming book on The Brewster Store.

BREWSTER: *The Way We Were*

MRS. PARKER'S TOURISTS HOME,   BREWSTER, CAPE COD, MASS.

postcard written on September 24, 1930

Across from the intersection of Route 137 and the Old Kings Highway is a multi-gabled house built around 1885 and originally owned by Reuben Clark. In the 1930's it was known as Mrs. Parker's Tourist Home and in the forties "White Gables." The charge for a night visit to Mrs. Parker's in 1930 was $1.50 per person. The house is now part of the Shady Knolls Camp Grounds. Behind it on the right hand side of the picture is the chimney of the house next door known as Brickenda (all the walls are brick) built around 1800.

The Queen Anne style Town Hall, pictured above, was completed in 1881 at a cost of $10,000. This old post-card was posted in 1909. When originally constructed the front porch was actually a porte-cochere for horse-drawn carriages. At right is a picture of the building from a 1930's postcard which illustrates changes made over the years. The original chimney was removed and replaced with a small roof vent. The small windows in the tower were covered; the roof cap was raised allowing room for a bell. Now the home of the Brewster Council for the Aging, for a time it housed the Brewster Historical Society. The upstairs was the original home of the Cape Cod Museum of Natural History.

Latham's On Cape Cod, situated across from the Old Town Hall, was a popular restaurant in Brewster for many years after World War II. Built prior to 1859, the building was the home of Captain Elisha Bangs. Today this structure is part of the Latham School, founded in 1970 to serve special needs children.

LATHAM'S ON CAPE COD
AN INN OF DISTINCTION
BREWSTER, CAPE COD, MASS.

postmarked November 6, 1953

From 1972 to 2005 in a complex of six buildings surrounding a replica of a New England gas-lighted common, the New England Fire and History Museum displayed a collection of thirty-five antique fire trucks and artifacts. The museum also housed an antique 1890 "Schmidt Apothecary" a portion of which is now at The Brewster Store, and the "Hopkins Blacksmith Shop" (now located at the Drummer Boy Museum Park). The property was purchased by the Latham School in August, 2013 as a site for their future expansion.

The museum included many antique autos including the only existing 1929 Mercedes-Benz fire truck – pictured below.

While possibly from the 1940's, this postcard picture showing Cape Cod Bay and beautiful Cobb's Pond was an advertisement by Warren E. Burgess, the owner for "the new exclusive seashore development, (in Brewster Village) known as 'Breakwater Acres', highly restricted but a good place to live." Almost in the center is an area which used to be a ball field.

Main Street runs from left to right in the lower portion of the photo – from The Brewster Store past the First Parish Church, the Consodine House, the Elm Tree Inn across from it and by two houses, the second of which was the former home of W. W. Knowles and now the Bramble Inn.

The horse trough and pump built in 1902 was donated to Brewster by Roland Nickerson and Herbert Woodworth. The small park area directly behind it served as carriage parking for the Congregational Church before it was converted into a park, "The Egg". Behind The Egg sits the home of Captain William Freeman, built in 1866. Previously on this site was the home of the Parson John Simpkins, third pastor of the Congregational Church. The Captain Freeman house was eventually converted into an inn known as "The Captain's Place Inn" and more recently the "Captain Freeman Inn."

FIRST PARISH CHURCH,
BREWSTER, MASS.

The First Parish Church was organized on October 16, 1700 as the Congregational Church of Harwich. Thereafter, a meeting house was erected. Proving too small, a second meeting house was built at town expense in 1723. Despite several renovations and the addition of a steeple, with over a hundred years of use the building fell into disrepair and was replaced in 1834 by the current edifice. Towards the end of the Civil War the church joined with the Universalist and invited members of the close by Unitarian Church (now The Brewster Store) to join. The church building was entirely renovated in 2011.

Consodine House,   Brewster, Mass.

Beyond the church is the Consodine House (now the Brewster Inn and Chowder House), the former home of Dr. Rogers. It was purchased from his estate in 1895 by John Consodine. From 1903 to 1950 it was operated by Clara Consodine, Rogers' daughter, as an inn and rooming house. In the early years her husband, a blacksmith, worked in the stables next door. The inn was a popular dining place for both locals and tourists.

STREET VIEW, BREWSTER, MASS.

To the east of the Consodine Inn were the stables which housed the horses, school barges, and wagons used by John Consodine, Clara's brother-in-law. Mr. Consodine transported children to school and travelers with their baggage to and from the train station and their homes and cottages in Brewster. Several residents of Brewster Park have memories of John Consodine meeting their train at the Brewster Station. The building is now called the Wobbly Barn, housing an art gallery and store.

ELM TREE INN
BREWSTER 6 CAPE COD

Across the street from the Consodine Inn is this house built around 1830. It became the home of Charles Freeman, a commander of whaling ships. The house was purchased from Captain Freeman in 1863 and Miss Cordelia Keith, a relative, inherited the house from her father. Starting in the early 1900's Miss Keith took in guests and operated the home for approximately forty years as the Elm Tree Inn. The inn was home to many antiques – and the Old Magee Stove. It currently houses the real estate offices of Kinlin Grover.

This early undated picture of the Old King's Highway looks west toward the Consodine house and Knowles Store (not in the picture but at the top of the hill in the distance) when the road was still unpaved. However, phones had already come to Brewster as evidenced by the telephone poles.

Main Street, Brewster, Mass.

The lower picture, from a card mailed in 1911, looks west along Main Street (the Old King's Highway) toward the Consodine House. In the forefront to the left is the former home of Captain Bangs Pepper (now the Pepper House). Next to it is the former home of Dr. S. H. Gould–more recently operated as the oldest gift shop in Brewster. It was built prior to 1850 and may be one of the older homes in Brewster.

Chapel
Brewster Mass. 374

After selling its church building to W. W. Knowles in 1865, the Universalist Society was revived in 1878 by Reverend Asa Bradley and a new chapel was erected a quarter of a mile eastward on Main Street (now Route 6A). The chapel has been expanded over the years and now houses a home and Parson's Art Gallery.

South Brewster

The Old Colony Railroad came to Brewster in late 1865, the death knell for the packet ships plying the bayside waters between Brewster and Boston. The station was located across from the intersection of Underpass Road and the Old Chatham Road (Rt. 137). The South Brewster Post Office was kept at the station. George Hopkins, served as the first postmaster at the station as well as station agent. Richard H. Hopkins, was appointed in 1871 as his successor; Richard F. Hopkins followed his father in 1882. This post office was closed in 1928. The automobile led to the demise of the railroad in 1938. The railroad tracks were eventually torn up and the right-of-way paved over for the Rail Trail bike path.

Underpass Road, from Route 6A to Route 137 is named for the underpass below the tracks of the Old Colony Railroad. As is obvious, the road was dangerous and after the demise of the railroad, the bridge over the road was torn down and the road straightened. Today the rail trail crosses Underpass Road at almost the same spot.

No Bottom Pond,   Brewster, Mass.

The Old Chatham Road was laid out before 1682. It was paved with macadam after the towns of Chatham and Brewster received checks for $2,000 each in 1907 and 1902 respectively from Samuel Nickerson. About a mile to the east of the intersection of Underpass Road is No-Bottom Pond. This picture shows a farm in the distance and the land, like much of that on the Cape, denuded of trees for farming.

postmarked August 21, 1920

Street View,   Brewster, Mass.

This view along the Old Chatham Road between Underpass Road and Route 124 is much the same as it appears today, although the street is now paved. The stone wall has recently been extended.

Sheep Pond
Brewster
Mass.

posted in 1910

Although houses have since been built along its shores, Sheep Pond is still pristine and little changed from this picture on a postcard mailed in 1910. A large parcel of land on the pond became Sheep Pond Estates, developed by Ralph Guida, who owned the house and barn on Route 6A now known as The Strawberry Patch.

Often a favorite place to take youngsters, Bassett's Wild Animal Farm was located on Tubman Road between Routes 124 and 137. It was started in the mid 1950's by Buddy Bassett, who loved horses from an early age. Its animals often escaped and roamed the country side, sometimes surprising local residents. The Farm closed quite a few years ago.

The Collotype Co.

East Brewster

The first house on this site was a log cabin built in 1693, reportedly by the Elder Brewster and Chillingsworth Foster. The oldest portion of the current structure was built in the early 1700's for the grand niece of the Elder Brewster, Mary Freeman, and Chillingsworth Foster II. The 1850 map of Brewster shows it still owned by the Fosters. The Reverend Thomas Bickford lived in it during the early 1900's. Today it is the famous Chillingsworth Restaurant.

To the east of Chillingsworth and on the south side of 6A is the farm, farm house, and barn known as The Strawberry Patch. It was originally built before 1858 when it was shown on the Barnstable County Atlas as belonging to B. Harding. The porch on the house may have been added in the 1860's; it has since been rebuilt. By 1880 the property was owned by Mrs. Baker, her husband having died in 1876. By 1907 Watson B. Crocker lived and farmed there with an orchard and cows, selling milk to local residents. It was purchased in July 1941 by Ralph Guida and sold in 1962 to The Sea Pines School for use as a dormitory, class rooms, and horse stables. The barn became a gift shop in May 1971.

The Strawberry Patch

Sea Pines

School of Personality for Girls

Sea Pines is the Recognized Pioneer School of Personality

Happy home life; personal attention and care. Students inspired by wholesome and beautiful ideals of efficient womanhood. The Cape climate is exceptionally favorable for outdoor life. One hundred acres; pine groves; 1000 feet of seashore. Ponies; horseback riding. Hygiene and morals observed especially for results in health, character and initiative. Gymnastics, Music, Handiwork, Household Arts, French, German and Spanish by native teachers. College Preparatory, Cultural, Domestic Science, Secretarial and other courses leading to Personality Diplomas introductory to definite service. All branches of study under experienced and enthusiastic instructors. For booklet and further information address

Rev. Thomas Bickford, A.M., Miss Faith Bickford, Prins., P. O. Box S, Brewster, Cape Cod, Mass.

In 1902, Faith Bickford and her family started a summer camp for girls – Sea Pines. The camp was situated on her grandmother's homestead along the Old King's Highway in East Brewster. Her property stretched from Main Street to Cape Cod Bay. The summer camp quickly expanded into Sea Pines School of Personality for Girls, a full time finishing and college preparatory school for young ladies. The above picture and text are from an undated newspaper advertisement.

Sea Pines School,   Brewster, Mass.

1054. - The Sea Pines, Home School for Girls. - EAST BREWSTER, Mass.

THE SHORE SIDE, SEA PINES SCHOOL, BREWSTER MASS 26.

The Bickfords added many buildings to the Sea Pines School and enhanced the main structure, attaching long wings to east, west and north. A fire in the 1940's destroyed the east and west wings of the main building; they were never rebuilt and the school closed in the early 1970's. It is now the Sea Pines Inn. In 1971, the farm house and stables across the street, then owned by the school, were sold and the barn became The Strawberry Patch gift shop.

Group of Girls at morning drill.

BUNGALOW SEA PINES CAMP
E. BREWSTER MASS

Arms are held high at morning drill. This photograph is dated 1915 and is probably of the Sea Pines Summer Camp for Girls.

The Drill Team for the Sea Pines School for Girls was probably taken in 1912 although it is labeled 1915. Note the Catholic church in the background with its steeple under construction which was undertaken in 1912.

The first Catholic chapel in Brewster was established by Father George F. Maguire of the Diocese of Fall River. The Immaculate Conception chapel was dedicated on August 16, 1908 on Route 6A diagonally across the street from the Sea Pines School and next to the farm that today is The Strawberry Patch. Fathers of the Sacred Heart assumed responsibility for the chapel in 1909 with Fr. Eikerling as Pastor.

The front entrance of the church was enclosed and the bell tower was added in 1912 with a ship's bell donated by Thomas Saint, although it was later removed. Further additions included the east wing in 1931, the sacristy, and a bathroom in 1962, and the larger west wing in 1968. There was a full restoration in 1998-99 that included replacement of the bell. The missionaries of Our Lady of La Salette assumed responsibility for the parish in 1961 and built a much larger church in West Brewster in 1962 to accommodate the expanding congregation.

Immaculate Conception Catholic Church, Brewster, Mass.   LC6

(Photo by Hicks)   76206

H. L. Moore Co.

H.F. FOSTERS STORE, E. BREWSTER MASS. 19.

The top picture to the left is from an early 1900's undated postcard of H. F. Foster's Store. The 1906 Walker Atlas shows the store in the general location of today's Foster Square. Mrs. Mertis L. Foster became the East Brewster Postmistress on March 19, 1919, a position she held until 1957 while she operated her store.

Post Office, East Brewster, Cape Cod, Mass.

FOSTERS

This photo was taken somewhat later given the gas pumps in front. The difference in roof pitch and location of the chimney of the two buildings pictured here, as well as the distance to the road, suggests they were not the same structure.

FOSTER'S

DAILY and SUNDAY PAPERS

Groceries — Frozen Foods — Fresh Meats — Fruits and Vegetables

FOSTER'S, EAST BREWSTER, CAPE COD, MASS.

Many will remember the Gulf Station, the East Brewster Post Office, and the old Foster's Store in East Brewster which occupied the roadside of Main Street for many years. The top advertisement was dated July 14, 1951. The buildings were demolished around 1980 to make way for the current Foster Square. This picture is from a post-card mailed in the 1950's.

Post Office. E. Bre

Just beyond the intersection of the Old Kings Highway and Ellis Landing was this house built around the mid 1820's by George W. Higgins who married a sister of Rowland F. Crosby in 1822. To the left in this picture is the building that served as George Higgins General Store. His wind mill for grinding grain was across the street. It also served as the early East Brewster Post Office with Higgins as postmaster from 1826 until 1857, when he sold the store and moved west. Cynthia Norway took over as proprietor and postmistress until 1860, followed by John Robbins until 1862, when Captain Foster purchased the store and assumed those tasks.

In 1877 Captain Foster sold the store to Reuben Chapman. With his brother Joseph, the store became Chapman Brothers, dealers in dry goods, groceries and hardware. After the turn of the century the store building was moved across Main Street and is there today as a private residence.

The lower picture is a different view from the west of the Higgins/Chapman store (background) and the Captain William Low Foster House which eventually became the post office. Despite selling the store in 1877 Captain Foster remained postmaster until 1881. His widow, Emeline C. Foster, assumed the role until 1886. Then, Joseph C. Chapman, the store's owner finally became Postmaster, a position he held until 1905. The building on the right served as the East Brewster Post Office until 1919, operated by Emeline F. (Fawcett) Hamblin. Thereafter, Mrs. Mertis L. Foster assumed the duties as postmistress at her store to the west on Main Street.

Charles W. Cartwright

TALLY-HO BAKERY BAR, Route 6 A, East Brewster, Mass.

Above, a third view of the Captain Foster house from the early 1900's after the building housing the Higgins Store had been moved across Main Street.

Many years later The Tally-Ho Bakery Bar was located in the still existing building slightly behind and to the northeast of the Post Office in the Foster house.

Before one reaches the stone wall and pillared entrance to the Nickerson estate (in the background of this undated photo taken from the Old King's Highway), a concrete wall stood in front of the Nickerson house built around 1835 by Rowland F. Crosby. The home was a near twin of the house built to the east by his brother Nathan Crosby. Around that house Nathan's son Albert built the mansion "Tawasentha". When Matilda Crosby married Samuel M. Nickerson in 1858, it became part of the Nickerson Estate. It was called the Fieldstone Hall Lodge. It has subsequently been expanded. A Nickerson descendant, Frances Nickerson, owned and lived in this home until her death in 2013, when it was sold to Ocean Edge.

FIELDSTONE HALL LODGE. E. BREWSTER MASS. 25.

This is the house that was burnt of Mr. Nicker. and this automobile Berth "

Fieldstone Hall, an adjacent carriage house, and a stone tower were built in 1890 on a 48-acre parcel of land by Samuel Mayo Nickerson, a prominent local man and descendant of the Puritan settlers who came to Cape Cod in the 1600's. The hall was built for his son Roland C. Nickerson. This picture, from an old postcard, is of Roland Nickerson in his car in front of his original home. The photo was taken sometime before May 10, 1906 when the hall was destroyed by a fire. Roland died two weeks later.

FIELDSTONE HALL.
EAST BREWSTER, MASS.

The rebuilt Fieldstone Hall can be seen in this long distance picture taken from south of the railroad tracks looking north. In 1907, a year after the fire, Adelaide (Addie) Daniels Nickerson, wife of Roland, began rebuilding the house in more of the style of an English manor house than in the original Queen Anne style.

posted in 1910

Fieldstone Hall, East Brewster, Mass.

This early postcard is a closer view of Fieldstone Hall much as it looks today. The mansions and adjacent property were sold to the Order of La Salette in 1942. In 1980 the property was purchased by Corcoran, Mullins, Jennison Inc. and converted to Ocean Edge Resorts.

E.F. Hamlin

Old Mill, East Brewster, Cape Cod, Mass.

American Art postcard

postmarked August 28, 1937

While the Brewster Store's archives contain similar pictures of the old Higgins Farm wind-driven mill at the Nickerson Estate as early as 1906, this postcard illustrates the position of the mill relative to the hall, tower and carriage house. The wind mill was built in 1795, across Ellis Landing Road from the Higgins Store. Later on it was moved down Ellis Landing Road and then purchased in 1890 by Samuel M. Nickerson for his golf course.

It was relocated from the Nickerson estate to the Drummer Boy Park in 1974. In 1975 it was added to the National Register of Historic Places.

Just to the east of the Nickerson mansion on the Old King's Highway stands this house built prior to 1831. The Hurd Family owned it by 1858 and it came to be known as "Windy Bush", the home of Mrs. Anna Daniels (Roland Nickerson's mother) in the early 1900's.

The name Tawasentha, as the thirty-five room Crosby mansion pictured below was called, came from Longfellow's famous poem "The Song of Hiawatha". The home was completed in 1888 by Albert Crosby who had made his fortune in Chicago. After retiring in 1874 and honeymooning in Europe for ten years with his second wife Matilda, he returned to the small family Cape-style house in Brewster, built in 1830 and situated on two hundred acres. He constructed his elaborate Queen Anne style mansion with a long arcade style porch around the original family home. It featured 13 fireplaces, an art gallery (to the far left of this picture), and a 60-foot high viewing tower which was unfortunately destroyed in the 1938 hurricane.

"WINDY BUSH" RESIDENCE OF
MRS. ANNA DANIELS,
EAST BREWSTER, MASS.

THE CAPE COD INSTITUTE OF MUSIC, EAST BREWSTER, CAPE COD, MASS.   480

E. D. West Co.

CROSBY ART GALLERY.
EAST BREWSTER, MASS.

No. 1046 A.

PUBL'BY
E. F. HAMBLIN.
EAST BREWSTER, MASS.

Tawasentha's ornate interior housed Crosby's extensive art collection. After Albert's death in 1906 his wife Matilda opened the gallery to the public. The property also included a large "Beach House" with its third floor turret.

Crosby Art Gallery,   East Brewster, Mass.

Tawasentha became the Cape Cod Institute of Music around 1936-38, founded by Martha Atwood Baker, and was authorized by the State to offer degrees in 1939. Its students and programs were chronicled in several articles in *Life* magazine. A fireproof wall and doors separated the art gallery from the house. Subsequently the entire structure became a restaurant. During this time a fire started in the art gallery. The firewall prevented the fire from spreading to the remainder of the house.

The property subsequently housed Camp Seascape, a summer camp for girls, only to become abandoned to the Commonwealth of Massachusetts in 1992. It was leased to the Friends of Crosby Mansion in 1994. This non-profit organization has beautifully restored Crosby Mansion.

posted in 1975

Artview postcard Co.

Camp Wahtonah-Camp Monomoy for boys was started in Harwich in 1922 by Robert J. Delahanty (Captain Del) and Harriman C. Dodd, two educators at The Worcester Academy. It moved to Brewster in 1926. Camp Wono for girls opened nearby in 1939. In 1950 Mr. and Mrs. Delahanty took over the camps. In 1975 the two camps combined and Camp Monomoy moved to the Wono campus. The Camp Monomoy site to the east was purchased by the State and merged into Nickerson State Park in 1983. Subsequently that site was leased by the State to the Cape Repertory Theatre.

WILD ACRES, EAST BREWSTER, MASS. F4.

To the left is a view of the main house which is today the headquarters of Camp Monomoy in East Brewster. It was built as a summer home by Mr. McQuillen around 1910. In the early 1900's it was called "Wild Acres." This picture is from a postcard posted on September 12, 1944. Even then there was a large open field in front of the main house.

WINTER SCENE AT THE BREWSTER PINES, EAST BREWSTER, MASS.

An early undated postcard shows the house called "Brewster Pines" which stood at the corner of Route 6A and Crosby Lane. The Isaac Crosby House was built sometime after 1829. Matilda Crosby Nickerson inherited it from her family. Owned by his parents, Roland Nickerson died here two weeks after his Fieldstone Hall burned. More recently it was a nine room inn and rest home run by Walter Baxter called "Boxwood." While a home to special needs boys, it was destroyed by a fire in the late 1900's. A new house was later built in its place. The adjacent barn with its cupola and pilasters still remains, converted into a separate residence.

This 1931 postcard (to the right) shows the East Brewster train station, then situated near where the Cape Cod Rail Trail now passes under Route 6A near Nickerson State Park. Note the old car in the background on the left and the white flag requesting that the train stop for passengers and/or freight. Its use as a train station ended with the demise of train service in 1938. The building was moved to a road near Ellis Landing and converted into a private residence.

937 R.R. Station, East Brewster, Mass.

posted in 1954

H. L. Moore Co.

Until 1934, the wooded campgrounds of Nickerson State Park were part of the sprawling estate of Roland C. Nickerson and his wife, Addie. The Nickerson family was the largest private owner of land on Cape Cod. Their guests were often invited to their lodge on Cliff Pond to join in hunting, trapping or fishing in fenced-in areas around some of the ponds. In 1934 Addie Nickerson and her daughter, Helen, donated more than 1,700 acres to the State in memory of their son and brother, Roland C. Nickerson Jr., who died during the 1918 flu epidemic. In 1935, the Civilian Conservation Corps (CCC) constructed the first roads, campsites, parking and picnic areas near Flax Pond. CCC workers planted 88,000 white pine, hemlock and spruce trees.

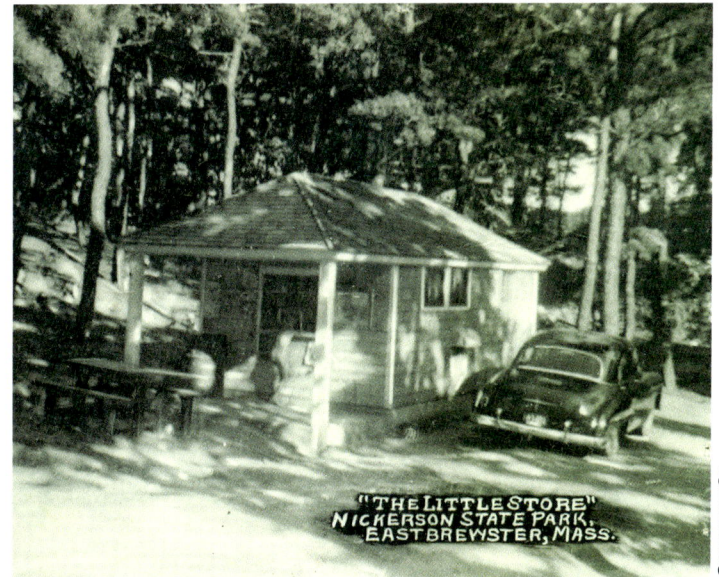

"THE LITTLE STORE"
NICKERSON STATE PARK,
EAST BREWSTER, MASS.

Garraway Co.

The Beaches

E.F. Hamlin

The Road to the Shore, East Brewster, Mass.

A postcard posted on September 8, 1913 pictures the dirt road to the beach in East Brewster, today called Linnell Landing. The main house of Linger-Longer-By-the-Sea can be seen in the distance at the edge of the beach.

Built as a private residence in 1907 the main house was shortly thereafter converted to an inn. It was sold to the Delahantys, owners of Camp Monomoy and Wono in the 1940's. Today it is still owned by the same family and operates as an Inn called Linger-Longer-by-the-Sea.

postmarked August 30, 1945

Linger-Longer-by-the-Sea, Brewster, Massachusetts

The Hancock Press

For those wishing to vacation on the beach in Brewster during the 1930's, renting a cottage for a week or two or even the whole summer brought great joy and fond memories. This postcard pictures a few of the many summer cottages that dotted the shore of Cape Cod Bay in East Brewster during the Depression. These six were at the end of Ellis Landing. Below is a 1991 aerial view of that beach.

ELLIS LANDING, EAST BREWSTER, MASS.

Eastern Illustrating Co.

postmarked July 20, 1933

Richard Cooper Kelsey

BLACK FISH, EAST BREWSTER, MASS.

postmarked July 3, 1934

From time to time whales have washed ashore on the beach along Cape Cod Bay. Early settlers prized these dead whales for the oil and meat that could be harvested. This black whale washed up on the beach in East Brewster.

SAILING ON CAPE COD BAY, CAMP MONOMOY, EAST BREWSTER, MASSACHUSETTS

Sailing has long been a tradition off the beaches in Brewster on Cape Cod Bay. This picture is of sailors from East Brewster's Camp Monomoy racing on Cape Cod Bay.

E. D. West Co.

SEA PINES, BREWSTER-ON-CAPE COD, MASS.

Swimming on Cape Cod Bay has long been a favorite of residents and visitors alike. The Sea Pines School for Girls maintained a dock for their summer camp from their beach in East Brewster as early as the 1930's. This postcard was published around 1952.

Cape Cod Souvenir.

F. R. & F. P. GOSS, HYANNIS.

Fish Weirs, Brewster, Mass.

Dear friend:—

How would you like to go to sea in a cart?

This weir is about one mile and a half from the high water mark. Sat. 1 P.M. Jan 26th 1906 Ellis

posted in 1906

Fishing was another source of food for residents. Lacking a harbor along the beaches of Brewster, nets were strung between poles called weirs to trap the fish. At low tide fishermen would go out in their horse-drawn carts to their weir nets on the Brewster flats and harvest the catch. Weirs were still in use on the Brewster flats until the late 1900's.

Pictured is the rocky beach front and some of the cottages on Clark's Point. It is now known as Point of Rocks Beach at the intersection of Point of Rocks and Foster Roads. Stone jetties were later installed and the beach became sandy. The three distinctive cottages were all built in the 1920's and still remain, although altered by subsequent owners.

Originally called Bath Street Breakwater Road, the site boasted a rock jetty harbor which was constructed for packet ships to dock from the 1840's to shortly after the coming of the railroad to Brewster in 1865. While it never lost its revised name it became a beach with a long row of bath houses pictured on this one cent postcard. Some of the bath houses were erected by Mr. Woodworth who then owned the house up the street which is now called the Captain Freeman Inn. Rent for the summer was $1 for the small bath houses and $5 to $7 for the larger ones.

postmarked September 1, 1907

BREWSTER: *The Way We Were*

Dear Blanche.
Kate working
over time Eating
clams, as fast
as Mrs Jones
can dig them.
Don't you think
I am an Expert
~~at~~ with my
Camera. —
Love to all
Bess.

Another favorite pastime on the beach was clamming. The plentiful supply of clams in the bay provided an important source of food for early Brewsterites. This photo postcard illustrates two clammers, one enjoying the fruits of her harvest.

posted in 1909

E.D. West Co.

Brewster Park was one of the first, if not the first, summer cottage colony in Brewster, having started around 1909. Brewster Park grew as people came from near and far to summer in Brewster and to enjoy its beaches.

posted in July, 1936

THE SHORE AT NO. BREWSTER MASS. 31.

This early picture of what is likely Paines Creek Beach contrasts sharply with the current view that greets visitors today. The curve in the creek is still there but erosion has sharply reduced the depth of the beach and eliminated the sea grass that once thrived there. Several cat boats can be seen afloat in the creek.

North Brewster

Franklin Crocker had been at sea early in his life, but returned to Brewster in his later years to operate a grocery store and post office on Brier Lane. It was located on the north side of the small triangle park at the intersection of the Old King's Highway and Stony Brook Road. It had previously been a tin shop. The building was purchased by T.D. Sears, who, in 1887, sold the grocery business to Franklin, who rented the first floor. From the outside his store looked very much like the Knowles Store. From the perspective of the Post Office System, this was considered the North Brewster Post Office and Franklin was its Postmaster. In 1915, two years before he passed away, the store was taken over by Curtis C. Eldridge. Franklin's son Henry worked for and then purchased the Knowles Store up the street. In the background can be seen the Captain Elisha Foster house, still standing today. The store building itself remains, but unrecognizable since long ago it was converted into a home.

In 1915 Franklin Crocker's wife, Mercy, was appointed postmistress of North Brewster dispensing the mail from her home on Stony Brook Road. In 1928 the North Brewster Post Office was eliminated and its duties transferred to the post office in the center of Brewster, located in the store of her son Henry Crocker.

Jay Hoops Studios

The Captain Isaac Clark House still stands today on Stony Brook Road, appearing much as it did when it was built around 1800 of fir timber brought back from Russia by Captain Clark. Although the document of separation of Harwich and Brewster was reported to be signed in its parlor in 1803, the agreement was actually signed in Boston. A copy resides in Brewster's Town Hall.

BREWSTER: *The Way We Were*

West Brewster

The original grist mill was constructed before 1665 through the efforts of Governor Thomas Prence. It served the residents of Harwich and Eastham, forming the beginnings of the Factory Village. This area also contained at various times a large tannery, a fulling mill to cleanse woolen cloth, and a cotton factory, all driven by the water falling from the lower mill pond down to Cape Cod Bay.

ORIGINAL GRIST MILL AND TANNERY, BREWSTER, CAPE COD, MASS.

The Collotype Co.

E. D. West Co.

The original mill burned in 1871 and was replaced in 1873 by the current mill on the site of the fulling mill with lumber from the salt works which is still visible from the inside of the mill. The Town of Brewster purchased the mill in 1940. The wooden water wheel and mill gears were replaced in 2012-13 and the dam supplying the water to the mill was rebuilt in 2014.

At left is a view of the old house across the herring stream from the grist mill on Stony Brook Road. A blacksmith is the first documented owner of the house. Only the rear foundation of the out building to the left of the house remains today. Recently sold the house is currently being restored.

The West Brewster Post Office (right) operated from 1826 to 1928; Mrs. Mercy and Mr. Eben F. Ryder were postmasters from 1860 to 1917. This photo was taken in 1912. The house was located on Stony Brook Road, east of the Dillingham Cemetery. It was most likely built by Roland Clark around 1800 and purchased at auction by Mr. Mark Clark in 1838.

posted in July 1913

WEST BREWSTER P.O.   WEST BREWSTER MASS. 37.

To better serve the parish which by the early 1960's extended to Dennis and Harwich, the La Salette Fathers purchased thirty acres of land on Stony Brook Road in West Brewster in 1961. Ground was broken in December of that year for the second Catholic Church pictured here. The new Our Lady of the Cape Church eventually proved too small and was extensively rebuilt and expanded again in 2004.

Our Lady of the Cape, R. C. Church, Brewster, Cape Cod, Mass.

E.D. West Co.

The photo on this postcard is of The Packet Antiques and Country Store on Stony Brook Road, possibly built around 1770. The sender described Packet's Store as selling "old fashioned candy, aprons, packaged unusual canned goods, and antiques."

posted in 1960

BREWSTER
MASS: BUILT 1690

posted in 1920

John Dillingham, one of the original settlers of Brewster and one of its wealthiest early residents, purchased his large lot in Brewster in 1668. His house, close to the road on the Main Street, is believed to have been built between 1660 and 1690. Possibly one of the oldest houses in existence on Cape Cod, the house is now in the process of being renovated.

THE DILLINGHAM HOUSES,   WEST BREWSTER, MASS.

The house next door, at the left in this postcard, was also a Dillingham house, built much later. It has since been moved to Barnstable overlooking Barnstable Harbor.

Sealand of Cape Cod on Route 6A in West Brewster was started by George Robert "Bob" King of East Dennis. This aquarium was home to trained bottle nosed dolphins, harbor seals, and Humbolt Penguins from Chile. When Mr. King passed away in 2011, Sealand was closed and today is a private home.

The Drummer Boy Museum opened in 1951 by Tony McGowan, who had purchased 17 acres on Cape Cod Bay. The museum housed many murals depicting scenes of the Revolutionary War. The lower picture to the left is of a mural entitled "The Boston Massacre". "Washington Crossing the Delaware" is at the right. When Mr. McGowan passed away, the museum closed and the property was sold to the Town of Brewster. A portion of the land was subsequently given to the Brewster Historical Society. The Higgins Mill and a blacksmith shop containing equipment originally part of the Fire and History Museum were moved here.

Originally housed in the old Town Hall, the Cape Cod Museum of Natural History on Route 6A has expanded from its modest inception in 1954. Today from its 80-acre campus beside Cape Cod Bay on Route 6A, the museum offers educational programs in marine science, environmental and ecological studies, as well as Cape Cod flora and fauna. The picture is of the entrance to what is now a 17,000 sq. ft. building.

The Nevin Orchard Lane Cabins were owned by R. A. and Eleanor M. Nevin at Betty's Curve on the corner of Route 6A and Paines Creek. It became a long-time landmark and featured twelve "modern" heated cabins with showers just one minute from the beach (Paines Creek). This 1930's photo is from an uncirculated postcard.

The Nevin
Orchard Lane Cabins--Route 6
Brewster, Mass.

E. D. West Co.

This photo of the Nevin Cottages is from the later 1930's. By 1941 the property was known as Orchard-land Cabins and Cottages and by the end of World War II it was known as The Jolly Whaler and Cottages. In 1946 the daily room rate per person had risen to $1.50-$2. per night (up from $1-$1.50 in 1941), while the weekly rate of a cabin or cottage was $20-$35. The property was sold to the Town which demolished Jolly Whaler a few years ago and the land has reverted to an unattractive lot rather than the lovely orchard it once was.

E. D. West Co.

O'DAY'S VARIETY STORE, BREWSTER, CAPE COD, MASSACHUSETTS 6064

TONIC·NEWSPAPERS·STATIONERY
Groceries HOOD'S ICE CREAM *Novelties*

O'DAY'S *Variety* STORE

ESSO

American Art Pos Card

postmarked June 28, 1928

O'Day's Variety Store and Esso Gas Station in West Brewster is pictured
in this postcard. Well-remembered by some older Brewster residents
but long gone, the site is now occupied by Luke's Liquors.

posted in 1909

The photograph on the postcard above is believed to be of one of two cottages built on Brier Lane by members of the Freeman family and can be dated to as early as 1725. Since this picture was taken, the house has been much expanded (as seen at the left) with the addition of a side porch and second story.

Brewster Park, a summer colony in Brewster, started around 1909 on property partially owned by W. W. Knowles; the property stretched from Lower Road to the beach on Cape Cod Bay. In its early years, summer visitors came by train from Boston, New Jersey, and other surrounding states and often stayed for the entire summer. The cottage colony slowly expanded as more and more visitors built small summer homes which were often expanded into year-round residences. Today Brewster Park is a thriving summer and year-round community.

postmarked July 24, 1924

Post Office and Store, Brewster, Mass.

Knowles' store served as a Post Office for most of the time between 1886 and 1936. His son joined the store in 1882 and it became W. W. Knowles & Son. The old curved top church windows on the front of the second floor were replaced around World War I—the only major refurbishment until 1989 when the structure was internally reinforced to strengthen the building and to accommodate retail use of the second floor.

STREET VIEW, BREWSTER, CAPE COD, MASS.   44105

MAIN STREET, BREWSTER, CAPE COD, MASS.

Henry T. Crocker worked for Willy Knowles before he purchased the store in 1926. He successfully operated it until 1945 as The H. T. Crocker Store. Crocker also sold insurance. When he purchased the store there was a small building housing an ice cream parlor to the east of the store. During the Depression the small building was moved down the street behind what today is the Parsons Art Gallery.

Henry Crocker decided to pursue his insurance business full time and persuaded his long time assistant Donald W. Doane to purchase the store in 1946. Donald, whose Cape Cod roots trace back to 1633, renamed it The Donald Doane Store. However, Doane's primary interest was in displaying his large collection of dolls and antiques in his museum on the second floor.

Donald W. Doane died suddenly October 3, 1970. The contents of the store were auctioned off and the building was purchased in 1971 by Faith and Robert Dibble, summer residents and owners of the Cedars General Store in Cedars, Pennsylvania. Robert is standing in front of the Store in the above photo. The Dibbles renamed the building "The Brewster Store" and repopulated it with general store antiques.

Their son, Tim took over as manager, selling coffee and newspapers, stocking many items normally sold in old general stores—such as oil lamps and molasses. After much debate with the Town, the Dibbles were able to reclad three sides of the building with vinyl while the front retained its original wood shingle and clapboard.

66

In late 1986 the Dibbles sold the Brewster Store to George and Missy Boyd who also owned the Strawberry Patch a mile to the east on Main Street. The Boyds restocked the store and added old church benches to the front court yard, creating a summer gathering place. In 1989 the first floor of the store was refurbished, adding new structural supports enabling the reopening of the second floor, rarely used since Donald Doane's Museum closed. In 1993 the Brewster Scoop, an ice cream parlor, was opened in the old shed in the rear. In 2005 the Scoop moved to the old post office building next door.

The back of the card at the back of the book . . .

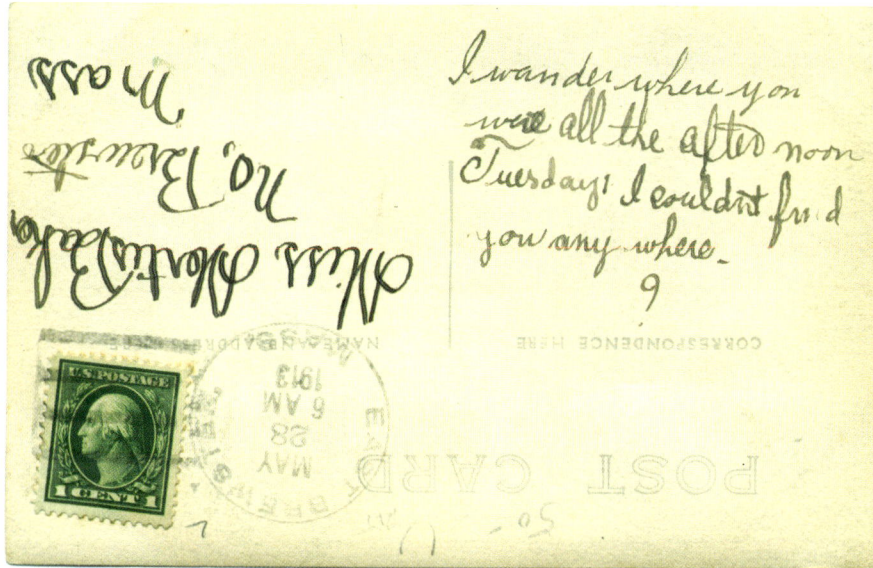

(Postcard 1, top left — addressed and postmarked MAY 28 1913)

Miss Martha Bell
No. Brewster
Mass

I wander where you were all the after noon Tuesdays. I couldn't find you any where.
9

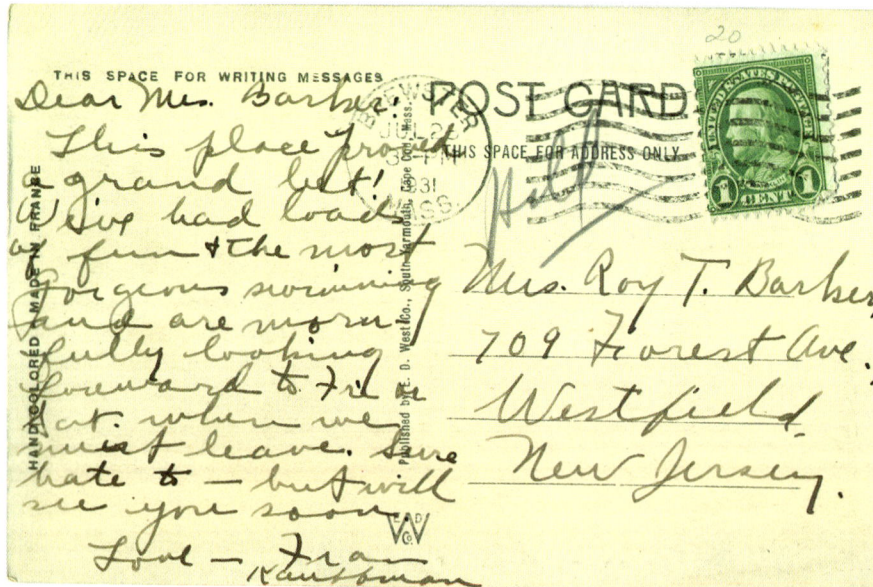

(Postcard 2, bottom left)

THIS SPACE FOR WRITING MESSAGES

Dear Mrs. Barker:
This place pro is grand but! I've had loads of fun & the most gorgeous swimming and are more fully looking forward to Fri. at. when we must leave. Sure hate to — but will see you soon.
Love — Fran Kaufman

Mrs. Roy T. Barker
709 Forest Ave.
Westfield
New Jersey.

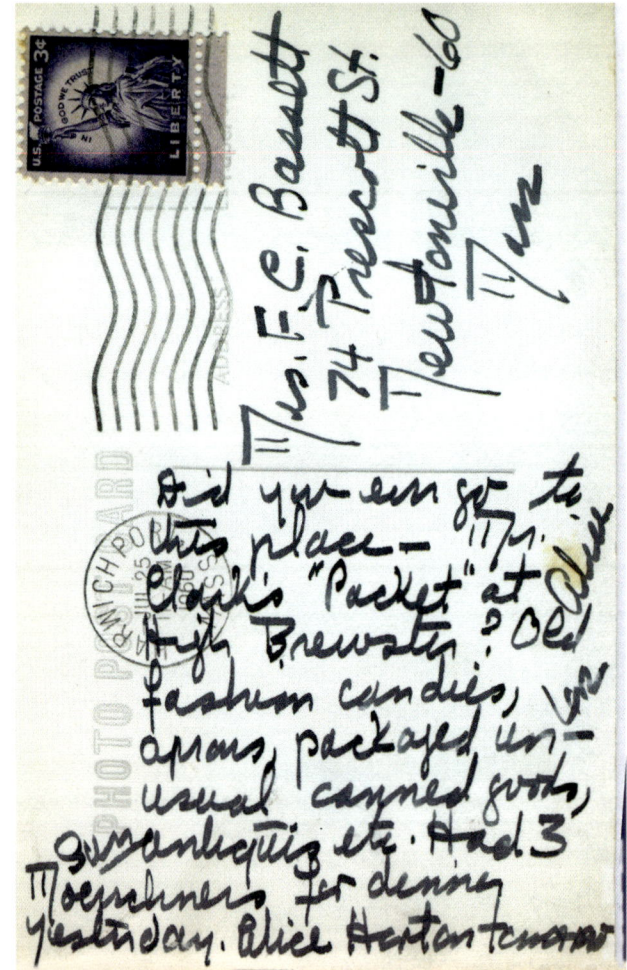

(Postcard 3, right — LIBERTY 3¢ stamp)

Mrs. F. C. Bassett
74 Prescott St.
Newtonville-60
Mass.

Did you ever get to this place — Mrs. Clark's "Packet" at High Brewster? Old fashion candies, aprons, packaged un-usual canned goods, antiques etc. Had 3 Foursomes for dinner yesterday. Alice Horton tomorrow